21 Ways to a

Happier
Depression

21 Ways

to a Happier

Depression

A CREATIVE GUIDE TO GETTING

UNSTUCK FROM ANXIETY,

SETBACKS, AND STRESS

Seth Swirsky

sourcebooks

"You've Got A Friend" written by Carole King
Sony/ATV Music Publishing LLC.

"Let It Grow" written by Eric Clapton
Warner/Chappell Music, Inc.

Published by Sourcebooks, Inc.
P.O. Box 4410, Naperville, Illinois 60567-4410
(630) 961-3900
Fax: (630) 961-2168
www.sourcebooks.com

Library of Congress Cataloging-in-Publication Data

Names: Swirsky, Seth, author.
Title: 21 ways to a happier depression : a creative guide to getting unstuck
  from anxiety, setbacks, and stress / Seth Swirsky.
Other titles: Twenty one ways to a happier depression
Description: Naperville, Illinois : Sourcebooks, [2017]
Identifiers: LCCN 2016044963 | (hardcover : alk. paper)
Subjects: LCSH: Depression, Mental. | Depression, Mental--Treatment.
Classification: LCC RC537 .S95 2017 | DDC 616.85/27--dc23 LC record available at https://lccn.
loc.gov/2016044963

Printed and bound in China.
LEO 10 9 8 7 6 5 4 3 2 1

Dedicated to my darling daughter, Daisy Claire.

"'21 WAYS' IS MY NEW BEST FRIEND: ACCESSIBLE, COMFORTING AND RELIABLE. AN INSTANT PICKER-UPPER!"

—ELYSE G., LIBRARIAN.

"THIS BOOK IS A MINI LIFE-SAVER. SHORT, SWEET AND VERY DOABLE ADVICE."

—IVOR D., AUTHOR

"DURING LIFE'S TOUGHEST DAYS, I OPEN THIS SOOTHING AND SAGELY BOOK."

—CARRIE ANNE S., SOCIAL WORKER

INTRODUCTION

You're depressed. I get it. I've been there. Almost everyone I know has been there, to varying degrees. For relief from the oftentimes horrific feelings that can accompany depression and anxiety, some of us take medication. Many of us see or have seen therapists. Some of us participate in the latest psychological treatments with important-sounding acronyms: EMDR, CBT, SE. We do these things in an attempt to make our depression lift. And yet, more often than not, that hazy, miserable, I'll-never-beat-this-terrible-feeling persists.

Instead of fighting it, I've come up with twenty-one small, simple, specific tasks that I've used over the years to help alleviate my own depression and anxiety-filled moments. I present them to you in this book. While they cannot cure depression, these tasks can help make the worst feelings a little less bad—and a little less bad, when it comes to depression, can be significant.

During my darkest times, using the tasks I outline here gave me needed respites, which gave me the confidence to face those feelings when they returned—and knowing that these tasks worked made me not fear the future. As a clinical psychotherapist, I now share the suggestions in this book with my own patients, who have been helped by them to a significant degree.

Depression and anxiety are very tough foes. If even one or two of the ideas contained within these pages can help alleviate your depression, then great—that's one or two more coping strategies than you had before. And as those of us who have battled the behemoth of depression or anxiety know, you can use any and all the help you can get.

Finally, one might ask why, in this day of easy access to information, we need this book when a person can just search online for "depression, help!" When you are feeling depressed, it's very comforting to have an actual, physical book around to flip through for a new idea or two, a reminder of all the little victories you can have. It's comforting and reassuring, like an old, trusted friend.

So let's get started. With this book, a happier depression is now, literally, in your hands.

Seth Swirsky, MA

1.

Paintbox

Sometimes I feel stuck. Like I'm in a box and can't get out. And I don't mean that literally—although sometimes I do find it hard to leave my apartment. What I mean is I get stuck in my own patterns and ways of doing things, stuck in communicating the same way about the same things with the same people. Don't get me wrong; patterns can be comforting and grounding, but they also keep me from having new thoughts and seeing and experiencing new things, which in turn keep me from moving forward in life.

During one of the times I was feeling boxed in, I thought I'd buy an inexpensive paint set, two brushes, and two small canvases. I didn't know what I would paint, since I'm not particularly visually artistic and I didn't feel like making a commitment to an art class. Still, something drew me to that art supply store.

At first I tried painting faces of people, which invariably ended up looking cartoonish, which led me to want to put away my new paints. But I noticed that I actually enjoyed the act of painting, the pushing around of paint on canvas with my brush. It was soothing, and it took my mind off my troubles. But what to paint?

I just started painting the simplest thing that came to mind: a box. I dipped my brush in the bright red paint and made a completely uneven box, then painted a few more red boxes on random parts of the canvas. Then I washed my brush and chose a warm butter yellow and painted more boxes. These new boxes usually abutted the red ones I had just painted, in a crashing, uneven way. But perfection was not the goal; the calming act of painting was. This was getting fun!

Lavender and orange and pink boxes, of all sizes, followed. And then I forgot to clean the brush when I changed colors and ended up inventing a new color that I'm *still* trying to name. After a few days the canvas was filled up, and as I looked at this color fest I had created, I found it pleasing to my eye. I then realized that a "good" painting is not necessarily determined by the mastery of the painter; it is determined by whether you can *feel* the painting. My colorful boxes (joined now by circles), in all their imperfection, felt alive to me—and made *me* feel more alive by having painted them.

THESE PAINTINGS ARE EASY
TO MAKE AND DEFINITELY WILL
HELP TAKE YOUR MIND OFF
YOUR TROUBLES.

The act of painting not only gave me a reprieve from the depressed feelings I was experiencing, but it also gave me a sense of accomplishment: I had made something that I now wanted to hang on my wall. A sense of accomplishment when you're depressed is so important in helping to alleviate the depression.

It turns out that painting boxes and circles—the most boring-sounding pursuit of all time—gave me peace, calm, and joy when I couldn't find them otherwise and is now a standard pastime when I'm feeling boxed in. Pun intended.

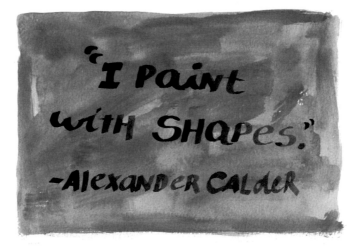

"I paint with shapes."
—Alexander Calder

NOThiNG BeTTeR THaN a LeTTeR

The simple activity of old-fashioned letter writing is relaxing and helps take your mind off of what's troubling you, even if only for the short time it takes to compose a letter.

Remember when you were younger and you sent a letter to a friend or relative in another city? It sounds like a lifetime ago, but outside of expensive long-distance telephone calls, letter writing was the main way people communicated with one another back then. Letters were fun to write, and it was even more fun to get one back! I would check my mailbox a few days after my letter went out in anticipation of a getting a return letter.

Letters are still a fun and special way to communicate with important people in your life. The excitement you get when tearing open a letter is the same feeling as opening a gift on Chanukah or Christmas. You'll be giving the person you're writing to a real thrill when they receive your letter; a personal, handwritten letter is no different from giving a gift. And who doesn't like getting gifts?

When I write a letter, I always try to use colorful stationery or one with a design on it to give it that extra touch. I put on some soothing music in the background, sometimes classical, but never pop, as the lyrics make me want to sing along and that distracts me from focusing on my letter.

Think of whom you would like to surprise with your letter. I remember discovering that my third-grade teacher was alive and living in San Diego. I got her address through the school where she'd taught me many decades earlier, and I wrote her a long letter reminiscing about the good times I'd had in her classroom, along with some other memories—like the time she caught me trading baseball cards outside her classroom and took them away from me! The memory made me laugh as I wrote it down; I knew she'd get a kick out of it. And wouldn't you know, five days later I received a six-page letter from her. She remembered taking my baseball cards and many other incidents as well. Boy, the gratification I felt reading (and rereading) her letter was palpable, and it just put me in a good mood.

I also wrote to some retired professional baseball players. I love baseball and its history, so I thought that writing to players from the era I grew up in would be a fun undertaking. I wrote to them through their old teams, not expecting to get anything in return. But when I got back several hundred letters from former ballplayers, you can imagine how thrilling that was.

In addition to the excitement of opening a letter, it's nice to connect or reconnect with people. In this age of instant communication—with email, texting, and the like—handwriting a personal letter to someone has great value; it's more personal, and it makes the person who received your letter feel valued because of the obvious effort it took to write it. Plus, your handwriting is a description of yourself, like a thumbprint. It's part of what makes you who you are.

Other suggestions for people you can write to might include a high school or college friend or a favorite aunt or uncle. Perhaps even a senator or governor whose views you agree or disagree with. It may take a few minutes to get addresses for some people, but I've found that you can connect with almost anyone these days with just a little effort.

Try and write letters on a regular basis, even if it's only one or two a week. It's a good discipline to get into and highly relaxing. Think of it as gift giving on a weekly basis, all for the cost of a stamp. Oops, wait... I think I hear the mail truck outside. Gotta go!

FiLiNG CaN LeaD TO SMiLiNG

A great sense of accomplishment comes when you are done throwing away the old papers and files you don't need anymore, and have made new files for the papers you have lying around. This is a daunting task, so daunting that most people don't take it on at all. Or if they do, they usually stop halfway through, because it's so hard to decide what to keep and what to toss.

I'm a bit of a filing genius myself, not because I love filing or have an innate ability to organize but because I've forced myself to do it enough times that I know I'm going to feel relieved, proud of myself, and happy when I'm finished. Also, I have a whole system in place that I feel makes this task as quick and painless as possible.

- You begin by making three different piles. The first pile has the obvious, no-brainer, important things you need to keep like insurance papers, passports, tax returns, and canceled checks. The IRS recommends taxpayers keep their federal tax returns and any supporting documentation for three years after filing; in California, it's four years for state tax returns. Be sure you know the rules in your state so you don't discard something you might need. Also, check with your bank to see if they scan your checks and make them available online. If so, you can discard those as well.

- The second pile has things you can definitely throw away. Again, these things will be obvious: old coupons that are no longer redeemable or newspaper articles that once interested you but now just take up space. You get the idea: chuck the stuff that has NO emotional hold on you.

- The third pile is stuff you can't decide on: old love letters, photographs, ideas for creative projects, info on that cooking class you were once interested in signing up for. This pile should be for things that HAVE an emotional hold on you, but by not sorting through each of those items now, you can still move forward with the overall goal of finishing the filing without getting bogged down.

● Now that you have your three piles, throw away your second pile, the stuff you don't need. Then, start to sort through the first pile and make individual files for everything you're keeping ("Insurance," "Tax Returns," "Health Care," etc.). This will be fairly quick and easy to do.

● You will be left with just one pile: the one with the "emotional" stuff. To keep it simple and not have to get into the feelings that many of the old photos or letters bring up, you might want to start a file called "Old Correspondence" and just stick those old love letters in there without reading them. Same for the old photos you don't necessarily want to look at right now but might in the future.

● Before you know it, you'll be done. As you put the files away in the filing cabinet or file box and take the trash out, you will feel lighter and more positive. You've cleaned out the past—what an accomplishment!—and made way for the NOW. Yay! Nice job!

Organizing your files has the added benefit of organizing your thoughts about the things you want to do and don't want to do in your life. Depression robs you of your clarity, but completing your filing restores it.

4.

LIGHTEN UP

We all know how light can affect the way we feel. A beautiful sunny day with clear, blue skies is more conducive to wanting to get up and go, excited about what lies ahead, than a gloomy day. If it's dark and rainy, I don't feel like getting out of bed, let alone leaving the house and going to work.

Just as outdoor light can affect our moods, so can indoor light. I found that the bright overhead light in my living room just felt so *blah*—similar to the way I felt inside. I didn't think I had any other option, so I just lived with it. Then one day I had a eureka moment and realized that if my living room lighting could affect me so negatively, surely there must be a type of lighting that would cheer me up! I was going to try to create a soothing mood instead of being at the mercy of that crummy light.

So I headed to the lighting store, looked around, and found some inexpensive table lamps that created the warm and comfortable mood in the store that I wanted in my home.

When I set the lamps on small tables around my home and turned them on, I noticed how calm they made me feel. Friends commented on how warm and welcoming my place felt. Some of the lamps have bulbs with three choices of wattage, so I can switch from a light bright enough for reading to that warm background glow I want when I just sit around or watch TV. Each lamp is warm and comforting by itself, but if you have several lamps in a room, turning different combinations on can create different moods. Try it! Who knew table lamps could be so much fun and help enhance your mood at the same time?

So if your home is feeling a bit dull or even too bright, change your lighting, and your mood just might follow.

"There's nothing more cozy comforting than the lamp lighting up a

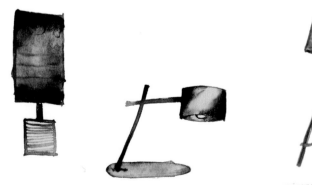

AND PSYCHOLOGICALLY GLOW OF a Soft table CORNER OF a ROOM."

— DR. Sandra SU

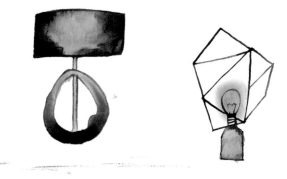

5.
Flower Power

Oftentimes people who are depressed hear advice such as "don't be so hard on yourself" or "try to love yourself more." Hey, that's not easy when everything feels so bleak. If you are unable to nurture yourself during those difficult times, you may find that taking care of a plant or two encourages you to take care of yourself.

Sometimes I feel as if I could use a little warmth, nourishment, and love, but it's not always easy to give that to myself. Maybe my confidence is a bit low; maybe I've had a rough week…or maybe I need the warmth, but I don't want to make it all about ME. Taking care of someone or something else is always a good option for these times, because then I don't make it directly about me—but I still find myself in a nurturing space, and that makes me feel nurtured and taken care of.

One way to cultivate a nurturing space is to plant something. It's easy, and it's fun right from the start, before anything has even started to grow. I get to go to the garden store in my neighborhood, where they have pots in all shapes, colors, and sizes. There's always a pot that makes me happy, and I know when I've found the right one because I imagine it in a place in my house, usually close to one of my windows so it can get the warmth and light the plant will need to flourish.

Then some soil. I try to go middle of the road here, because you don't need the expensive, supercharged stuff. Next, the seed can be any plant your heart desires, but to start, I recommend marigolds. Marigolds are known to be "easygoing," meaning they don't need a lot of work to grow. In fact, they bloom more in poorer soil, so there's really no need to worry about getting the perfect soil, and they grow rapidly and can survive in extreme heat, as long as you keep the soil moist. But most importantly, they are pretty and colorful.

Now comes the tricky part: the watering and the waiting. At first it's hard to be patient. You want that little sprout to bust through the soil right away! And it will, but not quite yet. The key is to have patience and to be consistent, and this part is actually where I find that the warmth and love come in. To take care of something, to give time and attention to it, to infuse it with

"PLANT
YOUR LOVE
and Let it GROW.
Let it GROW,
Let it GROW,
Let it
Blossom,
Let it Flow."

-ERIC CLAPTON

nourishment without an immediate benefit or reward, is empowering and makes me feel good about myself.

I work my plant watering into my daily routine, either before or after I give myself a shower, and BOOM! Before I know it, a little sprout pokes through the soil. Now I get to watch it grow. It's important not to claim a victory and slack off at this point, or to overwater, but instead keep up the slow and consistent watering…and talking to the plant, if you're like me and enjoy that sort of thing. Soon you will have not only pretty flowers by your window but also a sense that you nurtured a living thing to grow and flourish—and hopefully that will carry over to yourself.

6.

Yes!

When I feel sad or lonely, I don't feel like doing much. If I get invited to go somewhere, I usually say no, making an excuse for why I can't go on that hike or join friends for dinner. But the truth is, that's probably the time I *need* to get out more than ever.

So I chose to say yes to every invitation I received for one whole month, just to see what would happen. If someone invited me to go somewhere during that month—even if it was for an event at a later date—I'd have to say yes and put it on my calendar.

First, I was asked to go to a screening of an Italian film. A week later, I got roped into birthday drinks for a friend of a friend. On another occasion, my neighbor rang my doorbell on his way to a hockey game because he'd just gotten a call that his college buddy couldn't go.

OPEN YOUR
EYES TO THE
POSSIBILITIES.

GOODBYES
LEAD TO HELLOS.

TIE DYES
ADD COLOR TO
THE GRAYEST
DAYS.

19TH PRESIDENT
RUTHERFORD B.
HaYES
ONLY SERVED
LEMONADE
IN THE
WHITE HOUSE.

YESTERDAY
WaS.
TODAY iS.

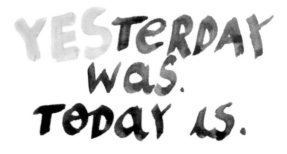

A yes and a yes and a yes and another yes later, I found myself doing things I likely would have made up excuses for not doing. I was annoyed at first to have to go to events I really didn't want to go to, but after I forced myself to say yes, I actually ended up finding something fun in all these new plans, and they sparked new friendships as well. That's something that wouldn't have happened if I had said no. Being engaged in these activities also helped me forget about any feelings of loneliness I might have felt at the time. Finally, doing these things gave me energy, and energy always helps lift your mood.

I gave this "saying yes" advice to a patient of mine, Marianne, a fifty-six-year-old single mom. One of the reasons she didn't like to go out was that she felt people found her boring and had nothing to contribute. So she stayed home alone and watched TV, feeling sorry for herself. But by saying yes and going to every event she was invited to, she learned that people liked being with her, which built her confidence. She stopped considering invitations to be "pity gestures" and saw them instead for what they were: genuine interest from other people in spending time with her.

I'm not saying you should force yourself to say yes to every invitation forever. But give it a shot for a month or even just a week. It might be hard at first or feel weird, but I promise you the strangest invitations will come along, ones that might lead to meeting new people and having a laugh or two. At the very least, going out will put your doldrums in abeyance, where they belong. Yes? YES!

7.

TO THINE OWN SELF BE...
COMPLIMENTARY

We humans are so hard on ourselves. Every day, the inner critic makes sure we know we're having a bad hair day, reminds us that the sweater we just spilled coffee on cost a lot of money, and even teases us for not having friends when we're feeling lonely. It tells us we're not making enough money or we're not fit enough or good-looking enough. Being human means living with constant reminders of failures, insecurities, and mishaps, even though most of us have daily victories worthy of praise and even celebration.

As hard as it is to disconnect from that judgmental voice, I've discovered a way for myself to feel good about the little victories that are part of everyday life: I give them their own voice. For instance, when I do something with my kids that I didn't necessarily want to do—such as driving them to the mall and picking them up—I say to myself aloud, when I'm alone, "You're a good dad. They really appreciated you driving them today." I say this often to myself because I make so many sacrifices for them, and every time I say it aloud, I'm giving myself a deserved pat on the back. Regularly acknowledging to myself my good deeds as a dad helps assuage my fear that I wasn't being a good-enough parent.

Because of the misgivings we all harbor about ourselves, it's healthy to compliment ourselves—out loud—when we succeed at even the simplest of things. Believe me, complimenting yourself on your little victories will help you appreciate yourself more and heighten your self-esteem.

When you make yourself a great meal, say out loud, "Wow, you're some serious cook!" When you clean your home and pay the bills, try "Just another day of being responsible!" Such affirmations go a long way toward helping you get a clearer, truer picture of who you really are: a person who does a lot of good things deserving of recognition. We compliment our friends daily for the little things they do; why shouldn't we compliment ourselves as well?

You know you did at least one thing today that was good and positive and worth recognizing and honoring. So, while it might feel weird at first, don't be afraid to give a compliment so that the most important person in the world—you—can hear it...out loud!

8.

A Gift Can Give a Lift

Every once in a while when I need a little pick-me-up, it always lifts my spirits to leave my house and buy something new—just for me. I'm not talking about a new car or a piece of jewelry or anything expensive. In fact, I find that the less expensive the item, the more I enjoy it.

As an example, there is a used-book shop pretty close to me, filled with a fantastic array of books on every subject imaginable. I usually find myself spending hours in there leafing through the old books. They remind me of when I was a young boy and used to sneak up to my Grandmother Mimi's attic, where she stored her vast collection of old books.

An old bookstore is a great place to find a gift for yourself on a subject you enjoy, usually at a very low cost. And why not? You deserve a gift, and it's nice to add something new to your home

"I always say shopping is cheaper than a psychiatrist."

-Tammy Faye Baker

as well. Every time you look at that book, you'll get a warm feeling remembering how you "found" it.

A key component of buying something new for yourself is that you not buy it online and have it shipped to you. Part of the enjoyment comes in being out in the world and bringing the item back into your home.

Along the same lines, there are many vintage shops around that sell off-beat antiques, vintage art, and knickknacks—many for very reasonable prices—and it's so much fun to browse the items! I once found a billiard ball with my favorite number—five—on it. I bought it for three dollars, and I love to look at it.

Some days I go to these places not knowing what I'm looking for and end up purchasing something I never thought I'd own. I recently bought a sundial from the mid-1800s. I put it in a spot outside where the sun rays align with it, and it actually tells me the right time, just as it did for its owner 150 years ago! It's a source of great pleasure for me and a conversation piece among my friends—and all for seventeen dollars.

So you see, you don't need much money to buy yourself something that will help lift your mood. You just need to find one of these cool, unique antique stores. A gift to yourself on occasion is a happy-making experience—and one you deserve!

9.

Late-Hour Shower

We usually shower because we just woke up or just worked out, or because we have to go to an important meeting or an elegant party and we want to look our best. Showers make us feel clean and fresh, of course, but they also make us feel "whole" again. A shower is an opportunity to feel and smell good, to get our hair just right, to feel like we deserve to wear that new, expensive shirt. A shower is about starting over.

How about showering just for ourselves, before bed? Sound luxurious? Well, it is. I know, because I do it. A lot. I shower not because I have someplace fantastic to go or someone new to meet and impress, but because showering feels good and because getting into bed in a clean pair of pajamas, with my hair wet, makes me feel cozy and clean and—yes—luxurious.

It also reminds me of being a kid. Taking a bath before bed

always calmed me down and settled me after a busy day of running around, and there's still something about that there for me: it's settling. Of course, I was much dirtier at the end of the day when I was a kid than I am now, but there's a sense of not getting into bed with the busy day still "on me." Instead, I've rinsed the day off and come to bed with a sense of completion. I've let the day go, both mentally and physically.

There's a newness that comes with this simple change in routine. I can sleep and dream from a place of being free and clear and clean. For me, at least, that means a night of solid, deep sleep. I wake up differently, too: I feel like a new human being, which makes it easier to get out of bed. So many benefits from something as simple as a shower!

Why a shower and not a bath? Baths are great, too, but a shower is quicker and easier. It doesn't require waiting while the bathtub fills; you just turn on the water and get in.

And while you shower, you have the opportunity to let go of your day. Let the water run down your body and watch it go down the drain, and while you do, think of the stuff you are letting go of. I like a shower just a tad on the hot side, but after about ten minutes, when my body is used to the temperature, I turn it one notch hotter. One extra little pleasure! Try it for yourself and get ready to feel clean and warm and fresh—just the ingredients for a good night's sleep. Don't underestimate the power of a nighttime shower!

"a relaxing shower can wash away the worries that occupy your mind making room for more productive thoughts."

-UNKNOWN.

10.

Lowering Your emotional Temperature

I used to suffer greatly from anxiety—"panic attacks"—with all of their associated symptoms. My heart pounded, my mind raced with all the worst thoughts; it was a nightmare. Those who suffer from anxiety will surely understand.

I tried different deep-breathing exercises over the years, but they did not help much. I read about and then tried all the calming exercises recommended by the latest mental health gurus, and while these may work for some people, they did not work for me.

After many unsuccessful techniques, I found something that *did* work for me. It not only brought me down from my panic episodes; it also worked when I recommended it to my patients who were depressed as well. And it couldn't be simpler: two wet, cold, wrung-out, and folded washcloths. You put one around the back of your neck and one on your forehead, covering your eyes, and then lie down. It is unbelievably soothing! Yes, drops of water *do* drip down your neck, getting your shirt and pillow a little wet, but that's a small price to pay for the true calm you'll feel. After about twenty minutes, when the washcloths get too dry, run them under the cold water again, wring them out (not all the way), and place them again on your forehead over your eyes and around the back of your neck and lie down.

High anxiety is like a high fever: you need to bring it down. While this idea of washcloths may sound "all wet," it's not. Sometimes the simplest home remedies are the ones that do the trick. Give it a try. I think you will enjoy the peaceful feeling it brings.

11.

TAKE A COFFEE BRAKE

When you're depressed, it's a very good idea to be around people, as I advise in chapter 6, "Just Say YES!" Hearing and seeing people interact can help recharge you. Rather than feeling *apart* from humanity, you feel *a part* of it. When you're down, you tend not to want to get out of your house. Depression plus isolation equals not such a good combination.

When I find myself heading down that path of isolation, I put the "brake" on my negative feelings by going to a coffee shop close to my home. Just being around people, observing them, listening to the various conversations taking place, perhaps having a little small talk with someone there, can lift my spirits.

Take your time; there is no rush to get back home. I bring my computer so I can get a few things done. Sometimes I take my bills and pay them at the coffee shop. Why not? I have to pay

them anyway, and being in the presence of others makes me feel more "in the world." More attached. More connected.

There are other places you can go to just strike up a conversation and get more connected. An Apple store is one such place. It's fun to talk to the salesperson about the latest computers, and you don't have to go to buy, just to interact. I spent a few hours there the other day doing just that. Browsing books on your favorite subject in a bookstore is another way to strike up a conversation with like-minded people, and an art museum is a great place to casually meet other art aficionados while taking in some stimulating art.

An hour at the coffee shop or at a computer or book store—anywhere there are people you might connect with—is a good way to ease the isolating feelings of depression.

12.

Time's a Wasting: Start Cutting and Pasting

During the times when my anxiety levels were really high and I was in a very scared state, the activity that always helped calm me down was the simple cutting and pasting of saved articles and pictures that I'd stored away in a drawer.

I have always saved clippings about things that interested me—for example, anything to do with my favorite group, the Beatles; my favorite athletes when I was growing up; cool pictures of the way people dressed in "swinging" London in the late sixties. You get the idea.

Each time I clipped out an article or photo, I would save it in a special drawer or box. Then I would buy a blank book—one of those scrapbooks with empty, white pages you can find in any art supply store. At the end of every month, I would lay the articles and photographs out on my bed and carefully and neatly cut out each article and what appealed to me in each photo. Next, I would apply glue to the back of each clipping with a glue stick and insert it into the book. In a short period of time, I had this really neat book of interesting and compelling stuff, but most importantly, the act of cutting and pasting brought my anxiety way down.

To further help relax me, I'd light a nice-smelling candle and just snip away. When I was in a particularly dark mood, this activity never failed to calm my nerves. My scrapbook became a source of consistency, like a good friend I could depend on when I got into one of *those* moods. The neat arrangement of my clippings in my book made me feel as if my mind, and thus my mood, were a bit more ordered and organized as well.

It took about a year to finish each book, and I now have almost twenty-eight books. Over the years, I started adding ticket stubs of events I had gone to, reviews of plays I had seen, little doodles I had made, even parking stubs to remind me of the restaurant I had gone to on a particular night, plus anything else I found interesting. As an added bonus, I knew that these books would be unique family heirlooms one day.

I now make it a habit to gather magazine items I find particularly interesting: quirky photos, inspiring quotes, provocative interviews, funny headlines—and all things relating to the Beatles, of course!

As with many of the other activities in this book, this one also gives a sense of accomplishment: I created these cool books that were sources of pleasure to look at, over and over again. And as I've said a few times in this book, feelings of accomplishment, however small or seemingly insignificant, go a long way toward alleviating the negative feelings that contribute to depression and anxiety.

Working on each book will give you a sense of peace and pleasure, and the book will feel like a reliable friend to you. When
you're feeling low, don't cut and run; cut and paste.

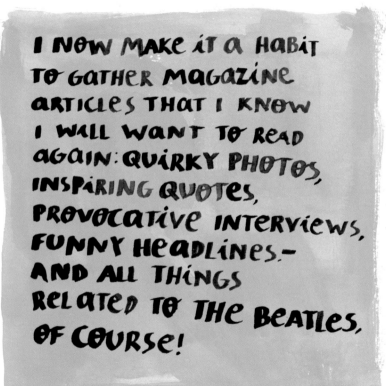

I NOW MAKE it a HABit
TO GATHER MAGAZINE
ARTICLES THAT I KNOW
I WILL WANT TO READ
AGAIN: QUIRKY PHOTOS,
INSPIRING QUOTES,
PROVOCATIVE INTERVIEWS,
FUNNY HEADLINES,-
AND ALL THINGS
RELATED TO THE BEATLES,
OF COURSE!

13.

HAVE SOMETHING TO LOOK FORWARD TO

When I have felt emotionally vulnerable, one thing that always helps is thinking about something I can look forward to later that day or night, like watching a series on Netflix. Reminding myself that there are episodes still to come gives me a short jolt of happiness and lets me know I won't stay in that dark place.

Favorite shows or movies are not the only things to look forward to. Perhaps there's a great Chinese restaurant that has food you love—and delivers it! If, when you're feeling down, you know you'll be treating yourself to a delicious meal later on, THAT is something you can look forward to for the rest of the day, and it's sure to elevate your mood.

How about a classic novel that you never got around to reading for some reason or other? Once you get into a great book, you'll look forward to reading it every night.

How about joining a book club or a movie club, where you meet like-minded people who enjoy the same things you do? You would look forward to going to these get-togethers every week.

"WE LOSE OURSELVES IN THE THINGS WE LOVE. IN THEM WE FIND OURSELVES TOO."

-KRISTIN MARTZ

Think hard about something you've always wanted to do and then learn how to do it. Quilting? Playing bridge? Learning to speak Italian? Joining a fantasy baseball league? Learning something that's special to you would be a source of enjoyment you can look forward to, *especially* when you sink into one of those dreaded, blue moods.

Depression keeps us stuck in our misery, and looking forward to a treat moves us into a feeling of anticipation. It may be minimal, but anything that distances us from the bad is good!

14.

PICTURE THIS: NEW PICTURES!

Sometimes my house feels dull or stagnant. When that's the case, it's hard for me to feel anything but dull and stagnant about myself. I walk though my house unconscious and zombie-like, with nothing standing out one way or another and nothing evoking my emotion. My environment has become bland and uninteresting, and, usually, so have I.

One way to enliven and freshen both my house and my mood is to update the photos I have in frames on shelves and on the walls. The idea is to replace the photos that don't give me *that feeling* anymore. You know the photos I'm talking about: they've been there so long you don't even notice them—and if you aren't noticing them, they aren't bringing you joy and happiness or adding anything to your environment. And a light and joyful environment can help in lifting your mood.

Having something new to look at in your picture frames is invigorating and adds to a sense of self-renewal. It's like updating your life. So take a walk around your house and ask yourself which photos are still relevant to your life. Are the friends you posed alongside still in your life? Does the photo of your brother and you going down the waterslide at Disney World twenty years ago still bring a smile? Or would that picture of you and your friends playing miniature golf give you more pleasure to look at?

Look through your photos on your phone or your computer—maybe you've overlooked a couple of fun pictures that make you feel good. Have a few of them printed out at your local print shop and slot them in a few picture frames around your house. You'll see how updated you feel, and feeling updated is always uplifting.

NEW PICTURES BRING NEW FEELINGS.

Remember, these pictures are for you, for your pleasure and enjoyment. They are not there to please or impress family and friends who come to visit.

Of course, guilty feelings may go along with this project. The guilt of taking down one of the fifteen photos of your children or displaying a photo of your sister but not your brother. Different photos will inspire you and make you feel happy at different times in your life, so chances are that the sibling or nephew or grandparent you left out on the last round will get a frame in the next go-round.

While most people don't have photos of themselves in frames around the house, if there's a photo of you that you really like, why not? Someone took a picture of me cheering at a baseball game. I look so happy in the photo that I have it framed on my desk. It reminds me that I have the ability to feel good.

While you're at it, take a look at the posters and paintings on your wall and see if you want to make any changes there. Sometimes an old poster can connect you to a past relationship in your life that perhaps is still unresolved. Don't be afraid to take it down and leave that wall blank until a new poster or painting that inspires you comes along. Until it does, a blank wall is just fine. Remember, every wall doesn't have to have something on it; sometimes it can be calming to have a blank wall, like a clean slate, a place waiting for something perfect to come along!

Updating your pictures can upgrade your mood. It doesn't all have to happen at once. Try replacing one or two and see if you don't get a sense of renewal.

15.

DON'T WAIT ON THE WEIGHTS

So many different things are required for working out: membership in a gym or a club; the right clothes and gear; a form of exercise that is challenging but at the same time not so hard that you give up; and most of all, motivation to leave your house and just do it. But it's a known fact that doing some form of exercise every day works wonders not only for your body but also for your brain and even your soul. At least it does for me; the stronger I feel physically, the more emotionally strong I feel as well.

When I do something physical, I feel happy; I've accomplished something. And you don't have to become a member of a club, buy a treadmill, or collapse your lungs inflating a giant ball in order to exercise. You don't even have to leave your home. I don't.

There's one thing you can do at home that will not only make you feel good about yourself but also increase your muscle tone. I'm talking about lifting weights. Not those heavy weights you can imagine a shiny, tanned body builder hefting while standing in front of a mirror and grimacing in pain. No, I'm talking about getting just one five-pound weight and one ten-pound weight (not a set) and starting slow and easy.

Begin with a few reps with the lighter weight, building your resistance and strength slowly, while you're watching TV or sitting around listening to music, or right after you wake up in the morning. For me, it's become the best way to start the day. Afterward, I feel happy and proud of myself, and it inspires me to try and accomplish more things throughout the day.

It might be boring or even hard at first, but muscle builds up quickly; the key is consistency. Soon enough, what was difficult becomes easy—and then too easy. That's when you move up to the heavier weight, and with it gain yet another sense of accomplishment. The goal is NOT to look like Arnold Schwarzenegger; it's to firm up a bit physically, which will help you "firm up" emotionally.

Two things to watch for are having good form and not moving to a heavier weight before you're ready. I learned this the hard way when I got a bit ahead of myself and wanted to build those muscles up fast...but now I know that consistency is the key. The way you know you're getting ahead of yourself is that you're using your back or shoulders or another body part to help lift the weight. Doing that stresses muscles and can injure them. So go slow at first. There should be no rush here.

REMEMBER, YOU SET THE PACE AND CHOOSE THE WEIGHT, AND SINCE YOU'RE DOING THIS IN YOUR OWN HOME, NOBODY WILL BE WATCHING OR JUDGING YOU. SO RELAX AND HAVE FUN... THE "WEIGHT" IS OVER FOR GETTING INTO BETTER SHAPE, PHYSICALLY, AND EMOTIONALLY!

16.

Box of Joy

Many people put their valuable items into a safe-deposit box. I think many of the most valuable items we ever get in life are not our jewelry or stock certificates but, instead, the warm notes we receive from friends and loved ones over the years, along with other personal keepsakes. These are the things that make us feel good and should be put in their own kind of box: a Box of Joy, where we can look at them when we're feeling down or need a reminder of how wonderful we really are and how much we mean to so many people throughout our lives.

I have my own Box of Joy at home—where I keep birthday cards, thank-you notes, personal letters, and every other good thing I've received over the years—that just makes me feel happy whenever I open it.

When you're decluttering your home and office, you're most

OPEN YOUR BOX OF JOY
AND FEEL BETTER.

likely to come upon these hidden treasures, and trust me, they will give you that warm, fuzzy feeling. Why? Because they said something kind about you or reminisced about a fun adventure or event you shared. There may even be a card from a former employer thanking you for revolutionizing the company's filing system, and that may make you laugh, not only because you disliked the job but also because you had no idea anyone had noticed. In short, rereading the notes in your personal and private box will remind you that you've been valued and appreciated. In spite of you feeling down, doing that is bound to lift your spirits and make you smile.

THEY ARE REMINDERS OF ALL THE ENJOYMENT AWAITING YOU IN YOUR FUTURE!

After you sift through all your papers and ferret out this feel-good stuff, make it a point to reread all the positive feedback you've gotten and then start to add photos to your collection, the better to connect the good thoughts to the people who expressed them. Add the rock from that hike you took with an old friend in Arizona, along with that seashell all the way from Tahiti.

It's good to keep your Box of Joy somewhere easily accessible, like the shelf under your nightstand, so you can visit it whenever you're feeling down or sad or alone and forgetting how highly you are thought of and how many good things in life you've enjoyed. They're reminders of all the enjoyment awaiting you in your future!

To make a Box of Joy, just find a box or an album or an old cookie tin and start to fill it with all the things that make you feel good—letters, cards, photos, rocks, shells, dried flowers, deflated birthday balloons, even bead necklaces from the third grade. And don't feel limited; it's your box, so you get to fill it with whatever fills your heart with good feelings. The only rule is that when you open it, you get *that* feeling immediately. Does it make you smile, giggle, or even laugh out loud? If so, you're on the right track!

"I WALK DOWN
MEMORY LANE
Because of all
THE HAPPINESS
I CAN RUN INTO."

-UNKNOWN

17.

Night at the Museum

Weekends can be tricky, because if I'm feeling depressed, I won't make any plans; and if I don't have plans, I'll most likely spend the whole weekend by myself, perhaps even inside, and that doesn't exactly help me feel better. But I know from experience that doing something new and different can create new patterns of thinking and get me out of my rut.

One thing that is out of the ordinary and doesn't require much planning is visiting a museum. I don't have to dress up, it doesn't require a reservation, and most museums are free. At first thought, museums sound stuffy and boring: big, cold buildings with old artifacts you stare at and are supposed to get some significant meaning from. But there are so many different kinds of museums aside from the usual art and history museums. There are biographical museums about some really interesting people,

"GREAT ART IS GREAT
BECAUSE IT INSPIRED
YOU GREATLY."

-YOKO ONO

folk-art museums, maritime and military museums, science museums, music and film museums, and even open-air museums and living museums, which are basically parks with interesting buildings or statues in them.

So whether you live in Dubuque, Iowa, which has the National Mississippi River Museum and Aquarium, or Mexico City, which currently boasts more museums than any city in the world, there is most likely something interesting in your city or town that you haven't seen and might be worth checking out.

The trick to a museum visit is the actual getting up and going; the phrase "Just Do It!" comes to mind. It's always inspiring and uplifting to see something you've never seen, and too many people don't go to art museums because they think you have to "understand" art. Here's a little secret: you don't!

The secret to knowing what is "good" art? If YOU like it, it's good! Sometimes it's the colors an artist used; sometimes it's the subject painted that is intriguing to you. Whatever the case, museums of all kinds are filled with visually and intellectually stimulating artifacts. So give a museum visit a try. It's a nice way to be in a different world for a few hours and away from persistent negative feelings.

18.

A MADE BED STARTS THE DAY AHEAD

When you're feeling down, it's hard to get out of bed, no question about it. You make all kinds of excuses, but what's really going on is that you don't have the energy or the will to face the world. You finally do get up, but the morning routine is a slog, and some things end up not getting done—such as making your bed.

But making your bed is a must. It's the act that officially begins the day. You may have your cup of coffee or a shower—whatever your particular routine is—but making your bed should have top priority. It's a terrible feeling to come home from work and see that the bed isn't made. It's as if yesterday didn't end, and that is depressing.

When you're feeling depressed, every small chore *seems* much larger, and when a chore feels large, we tend to avoid it.

But making the bed takes less than forty-five seconds to accomplish. Forty-five seconds! Yet when you're depressed, it's the first of many things that don't get done that day.

This may sound simplistic and silly, but try thinking about what gets your bed made the quickest. I put the pillows back in place first.

Then it's simply a matter of straightening out and tucking in the sheets and blanket. Done. (Add in another twelve seconds if you have a blanket at the foot of your bed that needs folding and a few more seconds for putting a duvet in place.)

Now every time you enter your bedroom, you will feel refreshed. Right in the middle of the word "renewal" is the word "new." Making your bed every morning gives you a sense of renewal, and that is an ally in the fight against depression. Not many things you can do in forty-five seconds that can give you such a lift. Making your bed sets the tone for your entire day and also gives you a good feeling when you come home at night to a tidy bed.

Each day has a beginning and an end; making your bed begins the new day while symbolically closing out the old.

19.

LISTS FOR THE LISTLESS

Isn't it the worst when you start thinking about all the things you have to do and the list seems endless? It's depression inducing. The appointments you forgot to write down, the grocery shopping that needs to be done, the various pending work assignments, the car tire that needs replacing...the tasks pile up in your head, and the weight of it all literally brings you down. It makes you not want to—or feel as if you can't—do any of it!

Add to these the things we'd like to do but haven't quite gotten around to: working on our (barely begun) novel from decades ago, cleaning out the garage or attic, cleaning out the car. And any number of various other pursuits.

One way to counter the feeling of being weighed down by all these things you have to do is to make lists. I always carry with me a small spiral notebook with blank pages. Whenever I remember something that I have to do, I just add it to my list. Even the smallest task—"buy wrapping paper" or "remember that Thursday is Tonya's birthday"—I write it all down.

What's the benefit of this? Well, all those chores that float around in your head feel heavy. When you put them on paper, they become lighter, doable. *And you can cross them off.* Each time you cross off an item on your list, you feel a sense of accomplishment, and that makes you want to accomplish even more! Before you know it, you'll look at your list and everything will be crossed off. You will have taken the chores that were badgering your brain and made them attainable by putting them to paper. Cool!

SOMETIMES I EVEN WRITE DOWN CHORES, TASKS I'VE ALREADY COMPLETED THAT WEEK, JUST SO I CAN CROSS THEM OFF. SEEING HOW EFFICIENT I'VE BEEN GIVES ME A GREAT FEELING.

Getting into the habit of making lists and knocking out each thing on it, one by one, is the gateway to tackling the larger projects you've "always wanted to do"—writing that novel, cleaning out the garage, a myriad of projects. More importantly, it will replace that depressed "can't do" feeling with a positive "did it!" feeling. And the more we do, the less depressed we are likely to feel.

Now, go and buy that notebook. It should be the first thing on your list!

20.

TALK THERAPY

Calling a close friend when you're in an emotional rut can be very therapeutic. You don't necessarily need someone to give you advice on how to escape your rut; you need only a compassionate, understanding person to *listen* to what you're feeling. To be all alone with dark thoughts or sad feelings intensifies them; to share, with a trusted friend, what you are experiencing can take away the power of the negative feelings. Talking with someone who has an empathic ear makes you feel less alone in your suffering—and that, in itself, will alleviate some of the emotional discomfort.

What if the people you know who are good listeners aren't home? I go to the "voice memos" app on my iPhone and just start talking into it, dictating what I'm feeling right then and there. Nothing replaces a friend, but if one is not available, it

"WHEN YOU'RE DOWN,
AND TROUBLED
AND NEED A HELPING HAND —
YOU'VE GOT A FRIEND."

—CAROLE KING

still helps to *release* your feelings by voicing them, into either the aforementioned app or another recording device, such as an old tape recorder or a digital recorder. In short, just get those feelings out.

Remember, you're not necessarily looking for a friend who gives good advice. No, you want somebody who is a very good listener, who you feel really hears and can empathize with the depressed or anxious space you're in. Friends like this are invaluable.

You don't always need the answer to what is emotionally ailing you; just expressing your feelings to a friend will go a long way.

Hair Today, Gone Tomorrow

A lot of people feel a strong connection to their appearance and like keeping it the way it's been for years (think boxing promoter Don King). For me, it's my hair, but fill in whatever your "thing" is—maybe it's a certain style of makeup or a pair of eyeglasses. It feels comforting not to change whatever it is.

For this reason, my hairstyle had stayed the same for most of my adult years, not only because it felt comforting, but also because it framed my face in a way I liked. It was a bit on the long side for a man, but it had shape, and I got it trimmed regularly so it looked well kept. Styling it required no thought or effort whatsoever, because it was so automatic. My haircutter, Ally, teased me about it every once in a while by saying "What are we doing today?" when she clearly knew what we were doing. "Just a trim, but not too much!" I would respond, and we'd both smile. Then a couple of months would go by, and we'd do the same thing all over again.

Something happened the last time I was there, though, and it has changed and impacted my life in so many ways. When Ally said her usual "What are we doing today?" I said, "What do *you* think we should do?" I'm not sure why I said that; it just came out, and I think it startled us both because there was a moment of silence. And then she carefully asked, "Really? You want to know what I think?" I nodded. She smiled and said, "I think we should cut it off." I'd had a feeling she would say that. I'd secretly hoped she would.

There was no commitment for me to do what she said; it would have been perfectly acceptable to hear her idea and then say, "Let me think about that until the next time," and that would have been that. But something inside me just wanted to make a change, lighten up, do something different. So I said, "Sure. Let's do it!"

She started cutting my hair, a bit hesitantly at first, but as I nodded and encouraged her to keep going, she cut off more and more. I started to feel lighter with every snip of the scissors, and when she was finished, I loved it. I felt so free and happy…and, surprisingly, relieved. I wouldn't have said before the cut that my hair was weighing me down or keeping my appearance stale, but with most of it now off, I felt lighter and more attractive.

If you're like me and hair is your comfort thing, I invite you to shake things up by getting it cut. It will make you feel light and new, and trust me, friends and family will notice and are likely to love it. If it's something else in your appearance, I promise you, making a bold change will help you see yourself in a different light, elevate your mood, and let you know that change—initiated by you—is very empowering.

'CUTTING YOUR
OUTWARD SIGN OF AN

HaiR CAN Be an INWard CHANGe."
-DR. LACeY LONDON

CONTRIBUTORS

Original watercolor paintings and script by Kirsten Tradowsky. Kirsten is an award-winning, San Francisco–based fine artist. Her work can be seen at kirstentradowskyart.com.

Isabella Betatio book design and drawings, pages 16–17, 59.

Seth Swirsky paintings, pages 23–24.

ABOUT THE AUTHOR

Seth Swirsky has a master's degree in clinical psychology and practices in Beverly Hills, California. He's an award-winning songwriter, filmmaker, and bestselling author. A graduate of Dartmouth College, Seth has three children: Julian, Luke, and Daisy. His work can be seen at seth.com.